Jabez

A Beacon in the Midst of Tragedy

For
Floyd and Evelyn

Yours in Spirit
and Light

Diane Hendici

This book is the first in a series from

 Heartline Healing Center

Guidance for Living in the 21st Century

Jabez

A Beacon in the Midst of Tragedy

Diane Krytzer Guidici

Guidance for Living in the 21st Century Series

Jabez

A Beacon in the Midst of Tragedy

Published by Heartline Healing Center
Tucson, Arizona

© 2001 by Diane Krytzer Guidici
ISBN 0-97167-560-0

Designed & Printed by

West Press, Tucson, Arizona

Table of Contents

Dedication

This book is dedicated to those who died in the attacks of September 11, 2001 and those who die in it's wake. May their lives lived and lost serve as a beacon to the future and a step toward World Peace and Unity.

Acknowledgements

It has been quite an experience writing and publishing this little book. On one hand, it almost wrote itself and, on the other hand, without the wonderful gifts of time, expertise and critique of family and friends, it might never have gotten out of the computer. There are many that come to mind and a few I wish to publicly acknowledge and thank.

Dr. Mari Helen High, Fredric Gould, David and Diana Beers, are just a few of those who read the manuscript and gave me some much needed feedback and lots of encouragement. John D. MacArthur, who listened and shared and read and just kept giving, not the least of which was an introduction to Carol Bedrosian, the editor and publisher of *Spirit of Change*. Carol was both insightful and supportive in her critique, leaving me with an inner sense of hope about my work. Ingvi Kallen always keeps perfection in mind as we work together. My mother, Virginia Stultz Krytzer, and my sister-in-law, Irene Guidici Ehret, gave support and suggestions that bolstered me as I made my final run. Finally, my husband and soul mate, Dominic, whose love and support give me the freedom to be myself, in this book as in my life.

Preface

This is my first book. However, it is not the book I set out to write last summer, nor the article I started in the spring that still awaits completion. I have several pieces in some stage of development, but perhaps that is the dilemma of all authors and I am new at this process. September 11th changed everything.

The beginnings of this little book go back to June 2001 when my husband and I were walking through the airport on our way to visit family. As is customary when we have a few extra minutes, we stopped at the bookstore. I noticed a large display of a small book, *The Prayer of Jabez*, by Dr. Bruce Wilkinson[1]. At first, I paid it little attention, but the book kept drawing me back. Finally, I decided I was "supposed" to buy it. I am used to having books "reach out and grab me", so this behavior was no real surprise. I did wonder, however, why I was buying an inspirational book by a Christian Evangelist, as this is not where I usually hang my spiritual hat. I think of myself as more "eclectic new-ager."

During the trip, I read the book, cover to cover. I found myself questioning what Dr. Wilkinson said, but I kept after it. I was somewhat intrigued, and I practiced the *Prayer of Jabez* on a fairly regular basis for awhile. Since I had just left my job of eight years and did not have any idea what was ahead for me, I thought maybe the book came as a way to help me find some answers. For some reason, though, I just was not comfortable with it and I put it aside.

A few days after the attack on New York and Washington, D.C., I glanced toward my desk and saw Dr. Wilkinson's book. At that instant, I heard a loud voice within me telling me that I was to write a response to September 11th, using *The Prayer of Jabez*. I was a little taken aback, especially since I was just about to take a few minutes for meditation. Still, this "voice" continued to insist that this was what I was supposed to do, NOW! "Okay, I will," was my response. It was clearly guidance that was coming to me and I had no reason to argue, so instead of meditating, I wrote. By the end of the morning, the key ideas found in this book were formulated and recorded.

As I wrote, the words just seemed to flow. I never questioned whether or not they came from me. I did not have the sense that another being was channeling information through me, yet I had the definite feeling that I was in communication with a source of knowledge that was beyond me. It was as if I reached up into the universe and brought these ideas into an everyday reality. As I wrote, I noticed that the style and language I was seeing on the paper was not what I was used to writing. While much of my work is spiritual in nature, it does not have such a strong bent toward what I might call religious. I found myself using religious language as if it were the way I talked every day. In my daily meditations, new insights would be given to me that then became a part of the text. Some days, I hardly recognized my own writing!

When I first sat down to write, I envisioned a couple of pages. When I was further guided that I was to share it with others, I thought, "Okay, I'll print it on some nice paper and send it out," already feeling the risk I was taking. Since then, this book has taken on a life of its own. Divine guidance doesn't quit; it stays with you until it is satisfied that the job is done. I invite you to open yourself to this Guidance, as I have …

The Age of Nations is past.
The task before us now,
if we would not perish,
is to build the earth.

Pierre Teilhard de Chardin, 1881-1955 [2]

Introduction

The Times

On September 11, 2001, one of the most horrific attacks that the world has ever been witness to was perpetrated against America. In a well-laid out plan of terror, four commercial airliners were highjacked shortly after take-off and used as weapons to bring America to her knees. All the planes carried many passengers intending to fly cross-country; all were loaded with fuel; all were within one hour of the hijackers' intended targets. Two planes were flown into the Twin Towers in New York City and one into the Pentagon. Each Tower burst into a fireball as a plane crashed into it. Within an hour both buildings collapsed. The plane crashing into a section of the Pentagon destroyed it through to the innermost ring. The fourth plane crashed in a rural area outside of Pittsburgh, Pennsylvania, as passengers thwarted the terrorists in their attempt to take over the plane. America was stunned. Nearly 4,000 people were killed, including citizens from eighty countries. Not just America, but the world was in a state of shock. A group of Fundamentalist Islamic Terrorists gave their lives, claiming to be saving the Islamic World from the ravages of the Western World, most particularly the United States. Never has the world witnessed such a despicable act.

After the initial shock was over and the President and others began to respond to the tragedy, the talk immediately turned to war. America had been attacked. It was an Act of War and now America was at war. However, unlike other attacks the world has experienced, this was different. As much as it was a violent attack causing death and destruction, it was an attack born of an ideology carried in the minds of a conglomerate of radical groups, groups of terrorists that can be found all over the world. As they work for their cause in small groups, called cells, they live perfectly ordinary lives, living in neighborhoods, shopping in stores, sending their children to schools. They are unrecognizable as terrorists. However, when the time comes, a few of them give their lives to such abhorrent and cruel acts as September 11th, while others continue to plot and plan further terrorism.

As with the attack, the war is unlike any war the world has seen. It is a war against terrorism; it is a war to save humanity from a radical and violent minority filled with hatred, fear and darkness. It is not just America's war; it is a World War. Almost every country in the world has joined the United States in this cause. We do not stand alone, we do not lead alone, and we do not walk the pathway to justice alone. How we walk that pathway, as a country and as the world, will determine much about our future.

Americans, and citizens the world over, have come together to pick up the pieces. The outpouring of service and patriotism is beyond any other seen in all time. Blood, clothing, money, time, energy, the outpouring of gifts is endless. Groups of strangers come together, come to sing and pray and share. No one is left out, Christians, Jews, Muslims, Hindus, Buddhists, all the religions of the world and those who have no religious home. It is clear that the terrorists do not carry the goodness of Islam as they claim. They have shredded it and chewed it up and spat it out upon us as they dishonored God, Allah, with this evil act.

Our lives have been changed forever. No one will be the same; no country will be the same. Still, we are unsure where to step as we begin to put our lives back together; we ask what the future holds, how will our lives be changed, what is expected of us. America stands straight and tall, but a new demand is being made upon all that America represents. Even though we don't feel safe, we know we must stand back up, pick up the pieces of our lives and move forward. We cannot run and hide or bury our heads in the sand or act as if it is business as usual, nor can we lash out at our attackers, perpetuating the terror they brought to us. We must move beyond the security of our lives before September 11th. To do any less would be to give the terrorists the power they claim. Just as the New War is being defined, we must redefine what we are about, what we stand for and how we make that stance, individually and collectively.

1

The Beacon

In my time of meditation a few days after the attack, I was reminded of the Prayer of Jabez, found in the Bible, I Chronicles 4:9-10[3]. This short selection is found in the midst of what reads like the census of the ages, a chronology of the lineage of the chosen people going back to Adam. Jabez is singled out in Chapter 4:9 of First Chronicles due to his seemingly unique birth experience, as it is described by his mother. "Now Jabez was more honorable than his brothers, and his mother called his name Jabez, saying 'because I bore him in pain.'" This has set him up for his plea to God, as it is written below.

I am grateful to Dr. Bruce Wilkinson for bringing this small prayer to our attention.

While I do not agree with much of his interpretation, especially his "Christianization" of this Old Testament plea to God, I do recognize the prayer as a beacon, set there to help guide one's life, then and now. All through the Old Testament we experience the wonderful capacity of the Jews to "chat with God." Not only do they talk with God in a most natural and informal way, they stop and listen and then, when they hear the answer, they act accordingly. It is a conversation filled with reverence, acceptance of the answer and obedience to God's instruction. Jabez's prayer is such an example of this relationship. It is within this context that I see this prayer as meaningful, not just for our individual lives but, most importantly, as a guide for our country and our world. May we rise above the evil, not as "better than" or God's "chosen", but as keepers of the Truth, soldiers of Goodness, creators of Beauty.

And Jabez called on the God of Israel saying,
"Oh, that You would bless me indeed, and enlarge my territory,
that Your hand would be with me,
and that You would keep me from evil,
that I may not cause pain!"
So God granted him what he requested.

Yes, indeed, this prayer is piercingly relevant and now must be incorporated and acted upon in each of our lives, individually, as a nation, and as a unified world. I speak of God and within that one word I speak of The Great Spirit, Allah, Universal Truth and the many other names by which God is known. I am using the *New King James Version*, as I believe the word "evil," as it is used in this version of the Bible, is important in light of its frequent use in relationship to the most recent terrorist acts. (See *Biblical Notes*)

It seems that this short prayer defines both the relationship of Jabez with God and how

Jabez should live his life. He begins by acknowledging that God blesses him. He is clearly in God's service. It is not a question but a statement of fact. He goes on to acknowledge that God determines how much territory he is given for which he is to be responsible. Being a devoted servant, he asks God to make it even bigger, giving him has much as he possibly can handle. Jabez realizes that this is something he cannot do alone, so he makes sure God is going to stay close to him, hold his hand, not let him go, not let him be so overwhelmed by the size of the territory that he cannot complete his work. Jabez is very aware of the presence of evil in the world in which he lives. He seems to know that evil will keep him from his work, so he asks God to keep evil from him. Jabez asks God to help him keep evil at bay. Further, he not only asks that he be protected from evil, but that he would not commit evil acts, would not cause pain to another. And, of course, God, kind and just, grants Jabez what he wants.

In its simplicity, Jabez lays out a very straightforward course of action for a very difficult task. In order to fulfill his part of the agreement, Jabez is going to have to keep his relationship with God in good working order. God will bless him, give him greater territory, hold his hand and keep evil at bay. Jabez has to be watchful over all his actions, what he says, how he is with others and with himself. While he seems to be getting a lot of help from God, he must remember that he has a larger territory to take care of and in his care-taking, he must watch that evil does not become a part of him nor cause him to hurt another. It really is a tall order; God seems to feel Jabez is up to the task because He grants him his request.

How is this a beacon for our time? Do we not pray to God for exactly the same things as Jabez? We do believe that our country is blessed; it is so stated on the Great Seal of the United States [4] and on our money. Is not our territory much bigger than the physical borders we claim? As a country, we are constantly promoting freedom and democracy around the world. In fact, the issue of territory is one on the main complaints of the terrorists! Is God holding our hands? It is printed on our money and in our Pledge of Allegiance, "In God We Trust." How do we ask God to keep us from evil? We work very hard at righting our wrongs, at making our ideals a part of the fabric of our lives. We value the goodness for which America stands. Jabez made his final request, that he would do no harm. Do we not make a conscious effort to have just and fair laws, to not single minorities out, to protect our citizens from harm as well as fight for others' freedom throughout the world? And, do we believe that God has answered our prayer? Certainly. We are the beacon to the world as this small prayer is a beacon for each of us today. Just as Jabez had to become more responsible to God, America must be more responsible to God through her relationships in the world. As Jabez had to adjust his ways to meet the demands of God, America must do likewise and adjust her ways to meet the same demands of God.

2

America Is Blessed

"Oh, that You would bless me indeed,"

America has, indeed, been blessed. For many centuries, this land and all of her wondrous resources have served the people living here well. There certainly have been trials, many have been mistreated, evil has made its way into various parts of our society. Many have paid a heavy price for the misdeeds of a few, but even with that, America has become a great nation, a leader in the world, a beacon for the poor, oppressed, and disenfranchised. And, in many ways, America has been protected from harm.

On September 11th, something changed that caused America and Americans to sit up and take notice.

America was wronged physically, emotionally, mentally and spiritually, and the whole world was witness to these wrongful acts. Are we the first to be so treated? Certainly not, although this may be one of the most extreme of violent acts. Is this a blessing? No, not in and of itself, God did not "choose" that we should be attacked, as some would profess, any more that He would choose to protect us from such activity. But, He has given us the opportunity to turn that most horrific act into a blessing. For America to embrace this act as a blessing, we must redefine our position, our relationships in the world and, most importantly, our responsibility to ourselves and to the world. If we have been blessed as the strongest and most powerful nation in the world, how do we now identify our responsibility, and to whom are we responsible?

Certainly we have seen our way to promote democracy, to fight for human rights, to provide for those suffering from poverty across the globe. Now that we have been attacked, do we let that service to the world go? Does our sense of responsibility to others now end as we try to take care of our own? I think not.

Our own country is a reflection of the world. There is no ethnic, racial, cultural or religious group that is not represented. Being blessed means taking on more, not less, while continuing to set the example for others to follow. It is so easy to take the role of the aggressor here. After all, we are the victim of the attack, are we not? So we must show the terrorists how big and tough we really are, right? They cannot get away with attacking us, right? That is not what this is all about. If we are blessed, chosen by God to model the greatness of a democracy representing the diversity of the world and given the freedom to fully participate, then how must we be in this situation? How can we model this truth and still take appropriate action with the terrorists? We must first acknowledge our position of greatness and choice. America was singled out for this act of terror not just because she is the strongest, most powerful nation in the world, but more because she is the symbol for the world of many of the highest values for mankind. She represents freedom, democracy, acceptance, welcoming and sharing with the entire world, to name just a few of these values. But in our urgency to bring the terrorists to justice, we must not whitewash the history of American aggression in her own land and on other peoples. America has often failed to live up to her ideals because we are too busy promoting our own, self-serving agenda, at the expense of many in need.

No, America isn't perfect, her citizens have not created heaven on earth, but the ideals on which she was built are still the basis for the strength and principles of her citizenry. America has been chosen and with acceptance of that choosing comes commitment and responsibility. Being blessed means something quite different than fighting terrorism with more terror.

Being blessed means showing the way, demonstrating new ways to deal with terrorism. President Bush is right; it is a new kind of war and we must learn to fight a new kind of battle. There will be many fronts to this effort; we must look at terrorism at home as well as abroad. It is our responsibility to right our own wrongs here at home as we do battle in other countries to stop terrorism.

The very actions of the terrorists are being echoed every day as we allow our prejudices and stereotypes to energize our behaviors. We speak of our country as "under God", but that does not make it belong to any particular faith, culture or color. Do we not welcome the Jews, the Buddhists, the Moslems, the Hindus, the Hispanics, the Blacks, the Asians? Or, do we only welcome them when it is convenient to Us... whoever "us" is? We see hatred and darkness everyday, in our local communities, throughout our country and around the world. If we truly believe that we are blessed, then right action, at home and throughout the world, must follow.

3

We Carry the World

"and enlarge my territory,"

Yes, our territory has been enlarged. We now have the entire world as our territory. Citizens from over 80 countries were killed on September 11th. The attack was on the World Trade Center, a microcosm of the world. How much more could we have asked for? Terrorism is rampant everywhere; no country and no people are excluded from its wrath. Terrorist cells have been identified in at least 60 countries, including our own. Our territory is ALL; it is not the protectionism of "our private land" nor the infringement on other countries for our "self interests." As we exhibit our patriotism, as we gather ourselves up out of the dust, we must remember that the United States, the strongest, most powerful, is not just the victim but is, indeed, the Leader in this cause against terrorism.

As we approach terrorism on a global level, we must also recognize, admit to, and address the same terrorist issues here at home. We have a lot of work to do to clean up our own territory, rid ourselves of local terrorism and acts of hatred and violence. We must go after not just the physical attacks but also those aimed at our intellectual, emotional and spiritual freedoms. At the same time, we must see beyond our borders and embrace the enormity of the responsibility that has been placed firmly in our hands. We are charged with shifting an incredible force of darkness into the light, to be revealed for what it is and transformed into love. To do this, we must listen to the voices of dissent as well as those who stand with us. We must listen and understand what it is that has energized such fear and hatred, as the terrorists express. Only then can we begin to bring light to the darkness and bring about a world-wide transformation.

How large is our "territory?" Have we not moved way beyond our borders, our self-interests, to promote, to support the ideals of freedom, of acceptance, of the ideals of democracy in a free world? We are not about creating a "bigger America," a world that looks just like us. We are about creating global unity, a unity built on Universal Truth, Goodness and Beauty, a unity with the diversity that truly reflects the world. The acts of September 11th accentuate the task at hand. What a Mission we have been given!

The first order of business declared the acts of terrorism as intolerable, abhorrent to the sensibilities of mankind. This was quickly followed by the call for a Coalition of Nations in the name of peace and justice. What a hopeful sign it was to recognize that our territory cannot stand alone; that we needed to bring in our brothers and sisters to partner with us in the cause of fighting terrorism. This, too, will take time. While we have had allies helping us since our nation was born, we are not used to "sharing power" in quite the way it must be shared for this New War. We, as a country, must realize the interconnectedness between our territory and the territory of others. To build a world free of terrorism requires a new belief system around the concept of "territory." As many have pointed out, the World Trade Center was just that, the presence of the world within our borders. As we redefine our territory, we must necessarily redefine our response.

4

With God's Guidance

"that Your hand would be with me,"

This is the true gift of love. We have not been given this responsibility and this larger territory without guidance, without assistance, without love. We keep singing "God Bless America" and feel the pain and sorrow and anger and injustice. We end speeches with "God Bless..." We somehow act as if God is just ours. Does God belong only to America and the countries that agree with us? Spirituality is not confined within borders any more than God is. We follow many leaders, Abraham, Jesus, Muhammad, Buddha and others. The teachings go even further back in origin. There is great diversity amongst the many religions today. Yet, even within this diversity, the teachings are quite clear; there are many more places of meeting on common ground than there are differences in expressing God's Truth. Whatever name we use, whatever leaders or teachings we follow, God's hand is our source of Truth, Goodness and Beauty. God does not take sides! His hand is with all of us, whether or not we choose to hold it. He provides us with opportunities to confront darkness, misguided truth, hard-heartedness and ugliness. God leaves the battle to us. The difficulty comes when we try to define that battle. If God's hand is in mine, what does that say about my enemy's hand, about the battle in which we are engaged? If God's hand is holding our hand, that very act must direct our action. It means we cannot use the same darkness, misguided truth, hard-heartedness and ugliness to battle those attacking us; nor can we take on an attitude of self-righteousness. What we must do is align ourselves with God. To be aligned with God is to act on Truth, using this knowledge through open, loving hearts with an acceptance of the beauty of all life. We must acknowledge and we must act on the reality that we are not alone.

I am reminded of an American Indian story about forgiveness. A young man had killed his friend. The family of the murdered boy sat around the council fire deliberating the fate of the murderer. They had the power to punish him in any way they saw fit, including killing him. That is just what many of the family wanted, his death for the death of their son and brother. In turn, they each called for his death. Grandfather brought wisdom to the council, pointing out that to kill the murderer would not bring the young man back to life, so what should they do? When the killer was given his sentence, he was stunned and it changed all their lives forever. He was to live in the tepee of the dead young man, he was to tend to the dead man's horses, he was, in fact, to take the place of the one he killed, to be the son and brother he had killed. He became a devoted son, the model of a loving son, well known and honored throughout the tribe. The tribe forgave and punished in a single act of loving kindness. [5] Can any less can be asked of us?

As we think about the great mission of America, we realize that a great responsibility comes with our Nation's birthright. The mission of America is clearly stated on the Great Seal of the United States of America, "Out of Many, One." If God is to bless us, to give us his love, to hold our hand, then we are so charged to "hold the hands of many, as we are one." Also on our Great Seal it is acknowledged that God has favored our undertakings and charged us to create a "New

Order of the Ages". To do this, He has provided us with the knowledge, love and experience of beauty in order to fulfill this favor. To hold His hand is to accept this charge and all the responsibility that goes with it. *(See Notes on the Great Seal...)*

5

The Battle of Good and Evil

"and that You would keep me from evil,"

This is most difficult because a great evil was done to us. To be kept from evil is to be sure that we do not perpetuate the evil energy, that we do not thrust more evil action in the name of "stopping terrorism." God does not "protect" us from the darkness of the world, but He does give us the opportunity to face it squarely, to choose our response, to not let us become filled with the same hatred, fear and violence. How quickly some of our citizens are to judge and to strike out – at Moslems, at Arabs, anyone with dark skin or a beard, at men with turbans and at women with veils. I am reminded of seeing a woman of European descent screaming at a Native American woman, "Why don't you go home where you belong?" Yes, this seems absurd, yet it happens here in America every day, as it does across the globe! The "Ugly American" did not get his reputation without cause. This kind of irresponsible action, whether physical, verbal or psychological, brings the evil to us, into our lives, into our psyche. We must be diligent to not become the evil we hate. America has always seen herself as the proud model of freedom, a freedom as given and defined by God. Many have, and continue to, come here to escape the terrorism they experienced in their homeland. They come here seeking the freedom to worship, to earn a living, to raise a family and to live a good life based on the very high ideals upon on which this country was built. Are the newcomers any less than our forefathers who built the road upon which we walk?

So how do we react to the evil acts of September 11th? We must hold to that higher ideal upon which we have built this strong and most powerful country. We must not assume that all Muslims and Arabs are terrorists just as we must not assume that all Mexicans are lazy and come to America to be taken care of. We all know, at a very basic and rational level, that all people are fundamentally good, whatever their beliefs and actions. Beliefs and actions stem from a wide range of causes. Many beliefs and actions may, in fact, be quite harmful, evil, to ourselves and to those whom we wish to attack. We know a lot about such occurrences manifesting as spouse or child abuse, road rage, children bringing guns to school, organized groups such as the Ku Klux Klan, Skinheads and the Islamic Fundamentalists. How do we keep this evil from ourselves? It is both simple and extremely difficult.

First, we must watch our own behaviors, attitudes and language. As we begin to catch ourselves acting or speaking in ways we find unacceptable in others, then our task is simple, change the way we respond. Changing the way we respond, however, is anything but simple. We must put our hand in God's and then enlist the help of others, since deeply set behavior patterns are not only hard to see but even harder to change.

Beyond our personal control over our lives and how much evil we allow in or to be expressed, how do we, as a country, respond? President Bush talks about this frequently in his public addresses and, as reported, in private meetings. He tells us that we must have enduring patience. We must bring everyone possible to the table, see and treat terrorism as a world issue, address the related issues and develop a variety of means to go after the perpetrators. We, as is so often the case, recognize the evil that comes to us from the outside. What is more difficult is to recognize those of our own responses that are rooted in that same evil thought. Those thoughts are no different than those of the perpetrators of terrorism! The terrorists do not define their attack as evil, but rather as a Holy War, a Jihad for Allah (God). In the same way, we do not define our violent reactions as evil, but rather as a means to bring about justice as defenders of freedom. As we do not accept terrorism, we must not condone our own aggressive behavior, our refusal to look at the whole picture, our refusal to engage in meaningful dialog, our arrogance and self-righteousness. Evil is evil, no matter on which side it sits.

In large measure, we don't know yet what to do. It is a New War with New Rules. It is being written as we fight. What will keep us from evil is using the tools God gives us.

We must…

- ask for the knowledge and wisdom we need to combat the evil of terrorism in new ways,

- use love to sustain us even as the battle goes on,

- continue the mission of America, to create a free and loving world and,

- maintain a long-term commitment to Right Action.

This is how God keeps us from evil.

6

How Do We Fight the New War?

"that I may not cause pain!"

How must we respond to these evil acts? We must think and act differently. We have been given the ultimate opportunity to lead. We must lead from a place of Universal Truth, knowing that our truth must be based in a greater arena; we are so used to acting as if everything is black or white, good or evil, right or wrong, for or against the U.S. We forget that there are choices and while some of the choices may be better than others, none of them are all white or all black. Truth is simply what it is, without judgment. While we act on the side of the righteous, attacking the evil with a great force truly will not rid the world of further evil being committed. Another evildoer will simply step into the arena. How often have horrific acts been committed in the name of God? These kinds of acts have gone on for centuries. No, our response must be different, must be new.

Our response requires Goodness for it is not just the mind that goes to war, but the heart also. What is the condition of our hearts at this moment, are we "out to get those guys who done us wrong!" as if that will overcome terrorism? Do we want them, "dead or alive" as President Bush has suggested? What kind of path do we walk as we face our adversary? While we truly must stay with Truth, as best we know it, we must also lead from the heart. We are asked to forgive, not the deed, but the doer of the deed. This is to lead from the heart. It does not mean we do not act, but rather, it reminds us that how we act is of the utmost importance. Certainly, as we respond to these acts, there will be pain caused to many, to both the righteous and the evildoers. Many others will be caught in the crossfire, a husband, wife, child left while others can only be held in memory. Yes, there will be pain. However, in causing that pain, are we acknowledging our actions, are we basing them on an objective Truth, leading from the heart and honoring individual and collective Beauty?

God has given us Beauty, the expression of Truth and Goodness. As we go forward in our response, do we hold to the truth that all life is beautiful, that all human beings are made in the image of God? Is any one of us less beautiful because of his/her rage, fear, or pain? It is often said, "Beauty is in the eye of the beholder." Can we see beyond the terrorist's face, beyond the horrible rubble and suffering, beyond the aggression? The impact of our actions must result in a greater appreciation for all things Beautiful, the result of action based on Universal Truth delivered with Universal Goodness (LOVE).

7

A New Order of the Ages

"So God granted him what he requested"

An Ancient Prayer Comes Home…

The *Prayer of Jabez* is from the Old Testament of the Bible. It comes from a tradition that believes one should demand "an eye for an eye." But that same tradition is based in the Ten Commandments. Two of them are especially relevant for today's crisis, "Thou shalt not kill" and "Thou shalt not covet thy neighbor… nor anything that is thy neighbor's." (Exodus 20: 1-17) In Islam, it is said that if one is killed, the whole village is killed. Buddha taught the way of compassion and nonviolence. Jesus taught us to "...love thy neighbor as thyself..." (Matthew 34: 36-40) What is most important is that each of these teachers lived the life of their teachings. The Truth becomes real in the life lived. Is that not our way, now, to live the life modeled by our teachers? Is this any different than living the prayer of Jabez?

How do we do this, live our lives by the highest ideal? How do we link this short prayer even closer to our lives as Americans? How do we make a religious truth real in a personal and a national way? So often we have felt confronted by the separation of our spirituality, our national pride and our private lives. Each crisis calls us up short. This time, it seems different and many of us feel a new kind of response is needed. Based on the ideals of seeking spiritual truth and living spiritual lives in our secular world, we reflect on our purpose, as individuals, as a group and as a country. As a part of this reflection, we need look no further than to the symbolism of The Great Seal of the United States. On the front side is the Eagle and the statement "E Pluribus Unum", "Out of many, one." America is the only country truly built from and with a citizenry populated by all the countries of the world. I doubt our forefathers envisioned the incredible diversity that we have become, but they surely saw and understood the vision to which they spoke. On the reverse side one finds a pyramid. Again, with wisdom and vision, two statements complete this powerful symbol. "Annuit Coeptis", "God has favored our undertakings" and "Novus Ordo Seclorum," "A New Order of the Ages." God has favored our undertakings – we have been blessed with an abundance of riches, but He has also given us an enormous task, to create a *New Order of the Ages*! And, He has made it a true partnership. This isn't something God is going to do. It isn't something we are going to do by ourselves. No, it is something we are going to do with God's hand in ours. To really make this statement clear, the cap of the pyramid is separated from its body and it is filled with an eye, the "Eye of Providence" a symbol of the Creator surrounded by rays of light. It has been said that when America realizes her vision, the Eye of God will again be attached to the top of the pyramid. Our current crisis can move us closer to realizing this Vision.

Where do we go from here? What does all this have to do with any of us and our everyday lives? We are just small specks in a very large country on a bigger planet facing an enormous challenge. We ask ourselves, "how do I make a difference?" Just like Jabez, we each pray, but there must be more to it than that. If we accept the idea that we are blessed, that our territory has been enlarged, believe that God's hand is in ours, that we will not be taken in by evil, and that we will not cause pain, then we must begin to live these beliefs. Here is a <u>beginning</u> list of what we can do now, today, and every day for the rest of our lives.

1. Pray, talk to God, tell Him how worried you are, ask for His hand to be with you.

2. Ask God to provide you with guidance... and then, listen. When you get His guidance, act on it.

3. Using your imagination, send light out across the globe, into the darkest and most troubled parts of the earth, into the canyons, crevices, and caves, filling them with bright light. Send the light to all the troubled peoples of the world and especially, send it to the leaders of the world, whichever side they represent.

4. Search out the truth, do not believe everything you hear or see. The truth is true, no matter which way you look at it.

5. Tell your elected officials, all of them, in your city, county, state and in Washington D.C., what you think. Let them know when they are right and when they are wrong. Too often, we remain silent except to mutter in the privacy of our homes or complain with our co-workers, family, friends and neighbors. We must hold our country, our government and ourselves accountable. Dissent is not unpatriotic!

6. Transform the violence in your life; consciously respond instead of react. Pay attention to the language you use and your "automatic" behaviors, at home, in the car, at work, at the grocery store, where ever you are.

7. Look around and see where you are acting out of fear or hate or prejudice; ask why and what you can do to stop that behavior. Then, commit to changing it today and everyday.

8. Pay attention to how you are with children, teens and young adults. What is the model you are setting? Be sure your attitude, body & verbal language, and actions demonstrate how you want them to be.

9. Act from a place of love; let your heart speak to you, it will tell you what you need to do in any given situation.

10. When someone treats you with ill will, thank him/her for the opportunity to love and to learn. You will most often do this silently, but it will have an impact, especially when you do not react in kind.

11. See the beauty all around you; share it with others. The more you recognize the enormous beauty that surrounds you, the more you will see.

12. Talk to people; share with them the good and the not so good, help others and let others help you.

13. Continue with your giving, of yourself and of your resources.

14. Remember, this is a 24/7 activity.

15. Don't forget to laugh, to breathe, to see beauty, to accept your humanness.

The list is endless. There are so many ways each one of us can make a difference. We have seen much since September 11th, the ugly and the beautiful. We have experienced an incredible outpouring of gifts. It is the energy that forces us to respond to such a tragedy that we must incorporate into our lives. Oh yes, Jebez wanted a lot and God gave it to him. Are we any different?

The biggest of the challenges, to co-create with God and to make the vision of America real, means that we must respond in a new way to bring us together for a greater cause than to simply "win a war". We know we can win a war, but can we fight the greater fight of good over evil.

In days to come
the mountain of the Lord's house
shall be established as the
highest of the mountains,
and shall be raised above the hills;
all the nations shall stream to it.

He shall judge between the nations,
and shall arbitrate for many peoples;
and they shall beat their swords into
plowshares, and their spears into pruning
hooks; nation shall not lift up sword
against nation, neither shall they learn
war any more.

Îsaiah 2:2, 4 [6]

When I began my morning meditation, I had no idea where it would lead me. Instead of sitting in quiet prayer, I found myself at the computer. I had been given a rather stunning assignment! This work has stayed with me for many weeks now. I have been further guided to send it to everyone I can think of and ask everyone to read it and to pass it on. I do not know where this will lead or what next will be asked of me. My life has become one of active, waking prayer. This is but one small piece. I share it with you in love and light.

Epilog

Three Months Later...

I am saddened by the actions of my government. I have written to President Bush and sent copies of my letter to many others. I had hoped that the President would have listened to his own words, "it is a new kind of war", "we must be patient" and "it will take time, it will be a long war". No, the missiles fly and the bombs are dropped. The Great Power shows its force and has begun, not the New War, but just the continuation of what we have always done. I had hoped for patience. I had hoped for the building of a strong and active worldwide coalition. I had hoped for the collective wisdom of the coalition to provide leadership. I had hoped for a New Kind of War

But this is not what I see. It is not what I read about. It is not Right over Wrong. It looks as though a bunch of hot-heads are scrapping in the field, each one just as self-righteous as the other... Except, it is not a game and I fear there will be no winners. We will all lose. Today, we have moved into other means of terrorism, notably Anthrax, with others looming in the wings.

At the same time, I find myself reading thoughtful and provocative editorials that are questioning the policies, attitudes and behaviors of our government. I see full-page ads, signed by hundreds of every-day citizens, asking for new ways to fight terrorism while we continue to provide humanitarian aid to Afghanistan and others in great need. I see demonstrations, groups of Americans gathered in the name of Peace. Indeed, there are many speaking up; there are many efforts at trying to demonstrate acceptance of the followers of Islam while fighting the fundamentalist followers of Islam as perpetrators of terror. President Bush talks about all the support he has from the American public - well, yes, we all support U.S. action in stemming the tide of terrorism, but no, we do not all support the current aggressive and violent reaction of our government. Many of us believe in the power of Right Action, in the power of prayer, in the power of love over hate, good over evil. While the voices of those of us calling for new kinds of action have little power, are mostly ignored and often considered unpatriotic, as we gather to shift the current reaction to the crisis, our collective force will be heard.

I believe good will win over evil; even with my sadness at the current American stance, I am hopeful. My life has changed, changed for the better, as I bring a greater consciousness into my life. I pray for right action. I send loving universal light throughout all the troubled parts of the world. I believe that heaven on earth, nirvana, enlightenment, inner peace or whatever one calls it, is possible in our lifetime, on this earth. It begins with me -and you - bringing the collective will and energy together to shift the enegetic forces on our planet from hate to love, from fear to trust, from war to peace. It means being armed with Truth (knowledge), acting through Goodness (love) and seeing Beauty (the expression of Truth and Goodness). It means *living the Prayer of Jabez*. I do believe, in my mind, with my heart and in all I see, that our country, America, has been marked to lead this great cause. I believe in the Vision and the Mission of America, as it is stated on the Great Seal, and I am committed to working toward its realization.

I was guided to write this book as a framework to enable us to deal with the current crisis, as a way to connect with God in a very real and practical sense. Now that it is finished, I realize it is a guide for rightful living no matter the circumstances, whether in the shadow of a crisis or when life is good and rich and full. The events of September 11th and the ensuing War on Terrorism have brought much that is wrong, and much that is right, to a new level of awareness. Now we must bring that awareness into a new consciousness, an active and dynamic force, a movement toward life in its fullest sense. The Unites States has taken many forceful steps to stop the terrorists, as would be expected after such an attack. But that force must not become the substance of the War on Terrorism.

What is urgently needed now is for the United States to initiate a dialog with the Islamic World to address the root causes that led to their people's turning to terrorist activities. Such a dialog would be mostly at the non-governmental level - a broad cultural dialog is envisaged. We must begin to understand the religious, social, cultural and economic, as well as the political issues that have led us to the unrest amongst the Islamic people in many nations. It is only through mutual understanding, gained through dialog, that we can begin to work together to transform the drive of a minority that sees terrorism as a viable path. As with all meaningful dialogs, all parties to the dialog will be changed by the process. This dialog is a critical first step if we are to have a world where evil is held at bay, a world in which we do not cause another's pain. The "War on Terrorism" is but a point in time, the many lessons to be learned will last for many lifetimes. Let us choose the right lessons.

I am neither a pacifist nor a warmonger.
I love America, I love the world and,
mostly, I love God.
What I know for sure is that God loves us all,
equally.

Bibliography and Notes

1. Wilkinson, Bruce. *The Prayer of Jabez.* Sisters, Oregon, Multnomah Publishers, Inc., 2000

2. Teilhard de Chardin, Pierre. *Building the Earth.* Wilkes-Barre, PA.: Dimension Books, Inc., 1965

3. _____ , *The Holy Bible*, New King James Version (NKJV) © 1990 by Thomas Nelson, Inc. (I Chronicles 4:10)

4. MacArthur, Jr., John Douglas. Introduction to the Great Seal, http://www.greatseal.com, 2001.

5. Zukav, Gary. *Soul Stories.* New York: Fireside, Simon & Schuster, Inc., 2000.

6. _____ , *The Holy Bible*, New Revised Standard Version (NRSV), copyright © 1989, Division of Christian Education of the National Council of Churches of Christ in the U.S.A. (Isaiah 2:2, 4)

Biblical Notes:

In the course of writing this book, I came across many different versions of text for the verses I am using. As I read each one, I was aware of the differences in interpretation that might put different twists on the points I was making. After giving this serious thought for a time, I decided to choose the version that most clearly spoke to our current situation in the world and has relevancy to our times. For the benefit of the reader, I have included the text for each of the four versions I considered using. They are:

1. ____, *The Holy Bible*, Authorized (King James) Version, Westminster Study Edition, copyright © 1948, W. L. Jenkins, Westminster Press, Philadelphia. (Translation: 1611 AD)

2. ___, *The Holy Bible*, New King James Version (NKJV), copyright © 1990 by Thomas Nelson, Inc. (Translation 1885 AD)

3. ___, *The Septuagint Bible*, Charles Thomson Translation, Muses Edition, 1954. Reprinted 1999, Shekinah Enterprises. (Translation: 1808 AD)*

4. ___, *The Holy Bible*, New Revised Standard Version (NRSV), copyright © 1989, Division of Christian Education of the National Council of Churches of Christ in the United States of America. (Translation: 1952 AD)

For I Chronicles 4: 9-10 (I am including verse 9, as I believe it sets the tone for the prayer in verse 10.)

1. 9) And Jabez was more honorable than his brethren: and his mother called his name Jabez, saying, Because I bare him with sorrow. 10) And Jabez called on the God of Israel, saying, Oh that thou wouldest bless me indeed, and enlarge my coast, and that thine hand might be with me, and that thou wouldest keep me from evil, that it may not grieve me! And God granted him that which he requested. (KJV)

2. 9) Now Jabez was more honorable than his brothers, and his mother called his name Jabez, saying, "because I bore him in pain." 10) And Jabez called on the God of Israel saying, "Oh, that You would bless me indeed, and enlarge my territory, that Your hand would be with me, and that You would keep me from evil, that I may not cause pain!" So God granted him what he requested. (NKJV)

3. 9) Igabes indeed was the most honourable of his brethren. Now his mother had called his name Igabes, saying, "I have brought him forth Os-gabes [with sorrow]." 10) And Igabes called on the God of Israel,

and said, If Thou wilt bless me with blessings and enlarge my borders, let Thy hand be with me, and give me knowledge that I may not debase myself. Accordingly, God gave him all that he asked. (CTV)

4. 9) Jabez was more honorable than his brothers; and his mother called his name Jabez, saying, "Because I bore him in pain." 10) Jabez called on the God of Israel, saying, "Oh that thou wouldst bless me and enlarge my border, and that thy hand might be with me, and that thou wouldst keep me from harm so that it might not hurt me!" (RSV)

Isaiah 2: 2, 4

1. 2) And it shall come to pass in the last days, that the mountain of the Lord's house shall be established in the top of the mountains, and shall be exalted above the hills; and all nations shall flow into it. … 4) And he shall judge among the nations, and shall rebuke many people: And they shall beat their swords into plowshares, and their spears into pruning hooks:

Nation shall not lift up sword against nation, neither shall they learn war any more. (KJV)

2. 2) Now it shall come to pass in the latter days that the mountain of the Lord's house shall be established on the top of the mountains, and shall be exalted above the hills; and all nations shall flow to it. ... 4) He shall judge between the nations, and rebuke many people; They shall beat their swords into plowshares, and their spears into pruning hooks; Nation shall not lift up sword against nation, neither shall they learn war anymore. (NKJV)

3. 2) For in the last days, the mount of the Lord will be conspicuous; and the house of God will be on the top of mountains; and exalted above the hills: therefore all the nations will come to it. ... 4) And He will judge among the nations, and work conviction in many a people: and they shall beat their swords into ploughshares; and their spears into pruning hooks; and nation shall not lift up a sword against nation; nor shall they learn war any more. (CTV)

4. 2) It shall come to pass in the latter days that the mountain of the house of the Lord shall be established as the highest of the mountains, and shall be raised above the hills; and all the nations shall flow to it. … 4) He shall judge between the nations, and shall decide for many peoples; and they shall beat their swords into plowshares, and their spears into pruning hooks; nation shall not lift up sword against nation, neither shall they learn war any more. (RSV)

It is interesting to note that Charles Thomson, Secretary of the Continental Congress, 1774 – 1789, is credited for the final design of the Great Seal. He was active in colonial resistance against Britain for decades. It was also during this time that he was deeply involved in translating the Old Testament from the original Septuagint (Greek) into the first American translation. It took him 19 years to complete the work, which was published in 1808 along with his translation of the New

Testament. As one studies the meaning of each side of the Great Seal and reads the biblical text, as translated by Thomson, it is clear that there are deeply held spiritual truths undergirding the birth and the development of The United States of America. It is to this vision and strength that we must now direct our belief and our hope.

The complete bibliography information for this reference is:
The Septuagint Bible: The Oldest Text of the Old Testament in the translation of Charles Thomson, Secretary of the Continental Congress of the United States of America, 1774-1789.

First published in 1808, it was edited, revised, and enlarged by C.A.Muses, Ph.D. (Columbia), 1954. The Muses edition was reprinted in 1999 by Shekinah Enterprises. For more details: www.greatseal.com/committees/finaldesign/bible.html

The eagle holds an olive branch and arrows, symbolizing a desire for peace but the ability to wage war. The Mission is stated, *E Pluribus Unum*, Out of Many, One. The reverse side bears the Eye of Providence, representing God and declaring the country's relationship with Him, "God has favored our undertakings," *Annuit Coeptis*. The incomplete pyramid, dated 1776, represents the building of a new country in a new land built upon the vision, *Novus Ordo Seclorum*, A New Order of the Ages. Visit the web site for an in-depth review of the Great Seal, its history and its meaning. (www.greatseal.com)

About the Author

Diane Krytzer Guidici has been a spiritual seeker since a very young age, when she found that her church did not fulfill her hunger for a more complete picture of what one would call "a thirst for knowing." As a seeker, she has explored many religious doctrines to find those kernels of truth that link all religions and many spiritual practices. In this process she has developed a personal spirituality which brings together the wisdom of the great religious teachers with a deep faith in God.

Diane is co-founder of Heartline Healing Center with her husband and soul mate, Dominic. She is a licensed Marriage and Family Therapist with Master's degrees in Clinical Psychology and in Transpersonal Counseling Psychology from John F. Kennedy University, Orinda, California. Her training includes a number of disciplines with a specialty in Psychosynthesis (known as a "psychology with a soul"), an approach to growth that focuses on wholeness through the acceptance and integration of the many parts of ourselves.

Diane is a credentialed teacher and administrator, having worked in the education arena for 27 years. She brings a unique blend of experience and study in both healing and education to her work.